Günter Gerngross · Herbert Puchta

PLAYWAY 3

PUPIL'S BOOK

Unit 1

Back to school

1 **Listen and speak.**

1 CD 1/2

2 Listen and speak.

3 Listen and speak.

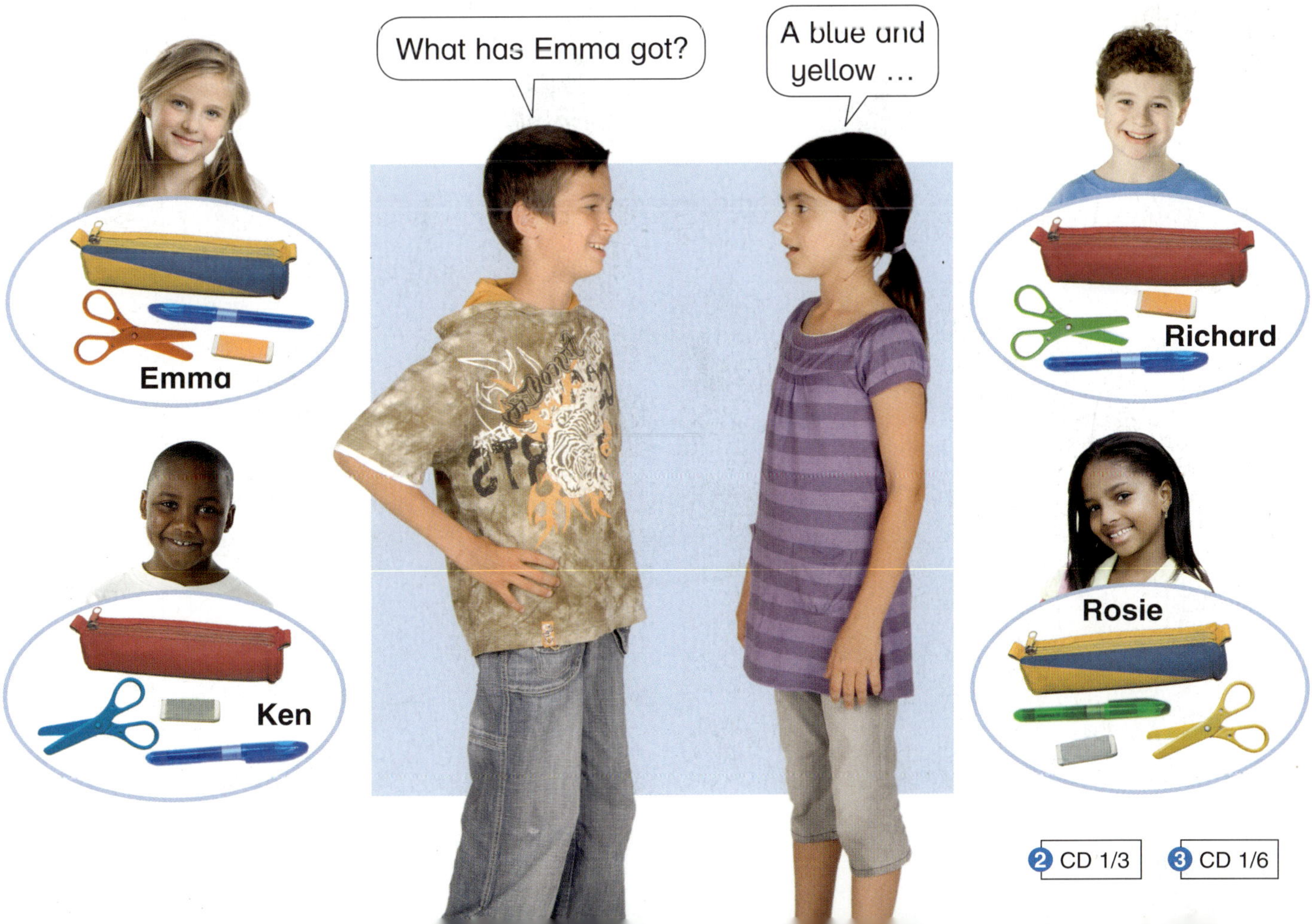

Back to school

4 Listen and point. Sing the song.

Oh, what a lovely morning

You're in bed,
and you wake up.
You check your watch.
It's time to get up!

Oh, what a lovely morning,
it's time to go to school.
Oh, what a lovely morning,
school is so cool!
School is so cool!

Wash your face,
put on your clothes.
Have a glass of milk.
Take your bag, and off you go!

Oh, what a lovely morning,
it's time to go to school.
Oh, what a lovely morning,
school is so cool!
School is so cool!

4 CD 1/8, 9

5 Listen.

Children at an English school

6 Speak.

Unit

2

Pets

1 Listen and point.

2 Test your partner.

3 **Ask five classmates. Take notes.**

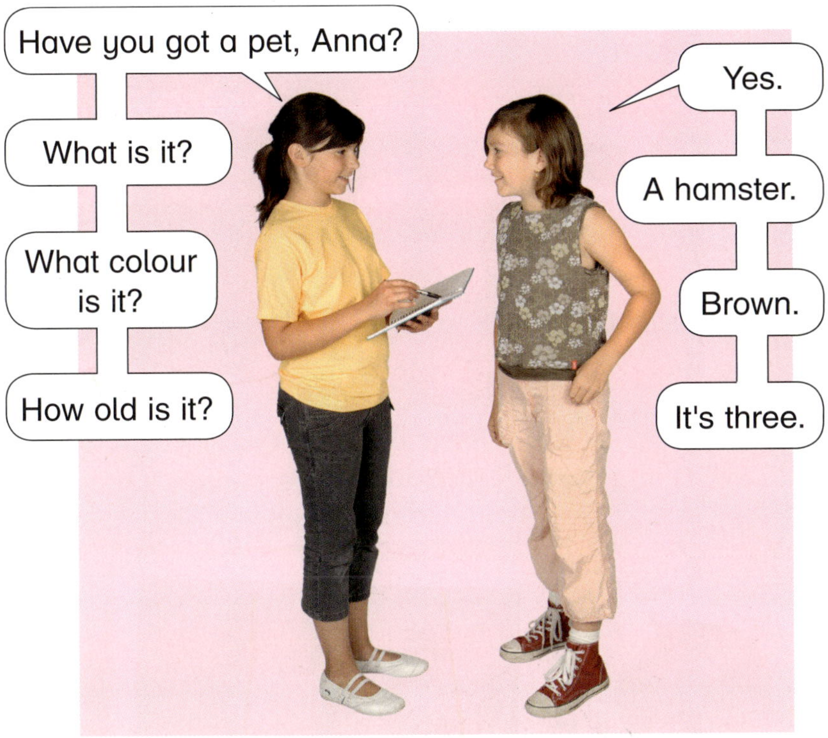

Name	Animal	Colour	How old?
Anna	hamster	brown	3
Peter	/	/	/

4 **Talk about your classmates and their pets.**

Pets

5 Listen and read. Then remember and speak.

Hi, I'm Justin. I've got a rabbit. It's eight months old.

Hello, I'm Ann. I've got a guinea pig. It's eleven months old.

Hi, I'm Laura. I've got a dog. It's two years old.

Hi, I'm David. I've got a budgie. It's three years old.

Hi, I'm Emily. I've got a pony. It's five years old.

Hi, I'm Jennifer. I've got a fish tank and twelve fish. They're sixteen weeks old.

5 CD 1/14

6 Listen. Sing the song.

Mice, mice, mice

Mice, mice, mice,
I like their little ears.

Mice, mice, mice,
I like their little feet.

Mice, mice, mice,
I like their little teeth.
Yes, little mice are really nice!

My mum hates mice,
my dad hates mice,
but I think mice are really nice.

I give them cheese,
I give them rice.
Yes, mice are really nice!

7 Read. Write your own text.

My text

I haven't got a pet.
My grandma has a budgie.
The budgie's name is Jimmy.
It's blue, yellow and green.
Lucy

My text

I've got a cat and a dog.
My cat is three and
my dog is four years old.
The cat's name is Socks.
The dog's name is Buddy.
Paul

6 CD 1/15, 16

Unit 2  Pets

8 Do the hedgehog quiz. Say "Red", "Blue" or "Green". Then listen and check.

1 What do hedgehogs eat?

2 What do they do in winter?

3 When do they eat?

4 How long do they live?

1–2 years	4–5 years	11–12 years

5 How many spikes have they got?

6 What are they scared of?

7 What do they do when there is danger?

6–7 Very good!

3–5 Good!

1–2 Try again!

8 CD 1/17

I'm scared

Unit 3

1 Talk in class.

I'm scared

2 Look and listen.

Culture Special

Trick or treat!

October 31st is Halloween.
Children in Britain and the USA dress up as monsters, witches or ghosts.

The children go from door to door.
They call out 'Trick or treat!'.

Most people give the children sweets.

3 Look and remember. Speak.

Note:
not scared
scared

	Lucy 	Michael 	Emily and Liz 	Thomas and Jeff 
	not scared	scared	not scared	not scared
	not scared	not scared	not scared	scared
	scared	not scared	not scared	scared
	scared	not scared	scared	not scared

I'm scared

4 Listen. Do the chant.

I'm scared

Are you scared of spiders?
Are you scared of frogs?
Are you scared of snakes?
Are you scared of dogs?

I'm not scared of spiders.
I'm not scared of frogs.
I'm not scared of snakes.
And I'm not scared of dogs.

Oh, really? Are you never scared?
Of course, I am!

I'm so scared of monsters
under my bed,
monsters in the attic,
monsters in the shed.

4 CD 1/22, 23, 24

5 Listen and point.

cake

fly

bear

rat

shirt

crocodile - a croc

house

6 Listen and speak.

7 Write your own rhyme and draw a picture.

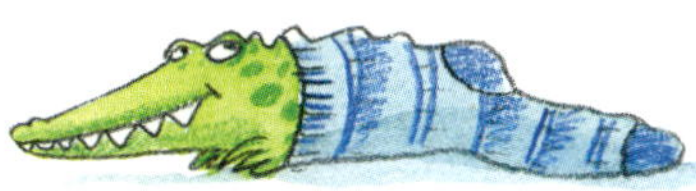
a croc in my sock

a bee on my knee

a rat on my hat

a bear on my chair

a mouse in my house

a bird in my shirt

a fly in my eye

a snake in my cake

Unit 3

I'm scared

8 **Read and act out. Create your own story.**

1

2

9 **Read. Write your own text.**

My text

I'm scared of spiders and snakes.
I'm not scared of dogs.
I like dogs.
But my dad is scared of dogs.

What's the time?

Unit 4

1 **Listen. Say the rhyme.**

Hickory ...

Hickory dickory dock,
the mouse ran up the clock.
The clock struck one,
the mouse ran down.
Hickory dickory dock.

2 **Listen and point.**

1

2

3

4

1 CD 1/28 2 CD 1/29

What's the time?

3 Listen and point.

cat

bat

dog

frog

fox

ox

mouse

louse

4 Listen. Do the chant.

5 Write your own chant. Draw a picture.

3 CD 1/32   4 CD 1/33, 34, 35

6 Play the game.

What's the time?

8 Listen and point. Act out the sketch.

The missing flowers

 8 CD 1/37

9 Listen. Find Tina, Christine and Sally.

10 Read. Write your own text.

My text

I get up at quarter past six.
I have breakfast at half past six.
I go to school at seven.
School starts at quarter to eight.
I come home at half past twelve.

What's the time?

11 **Test your partner. What can she/he do in a minute?**

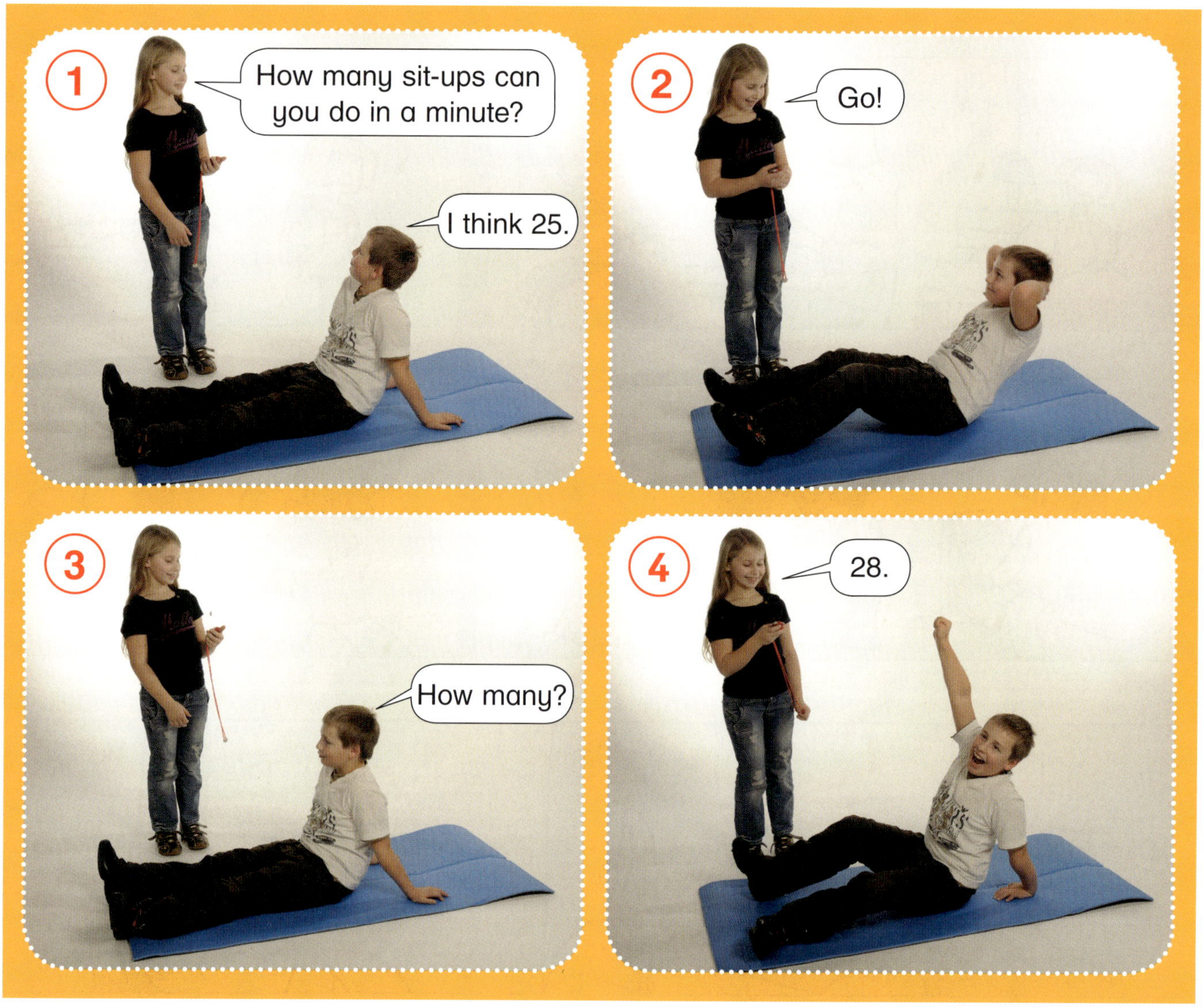

My body

1 Listen and point.

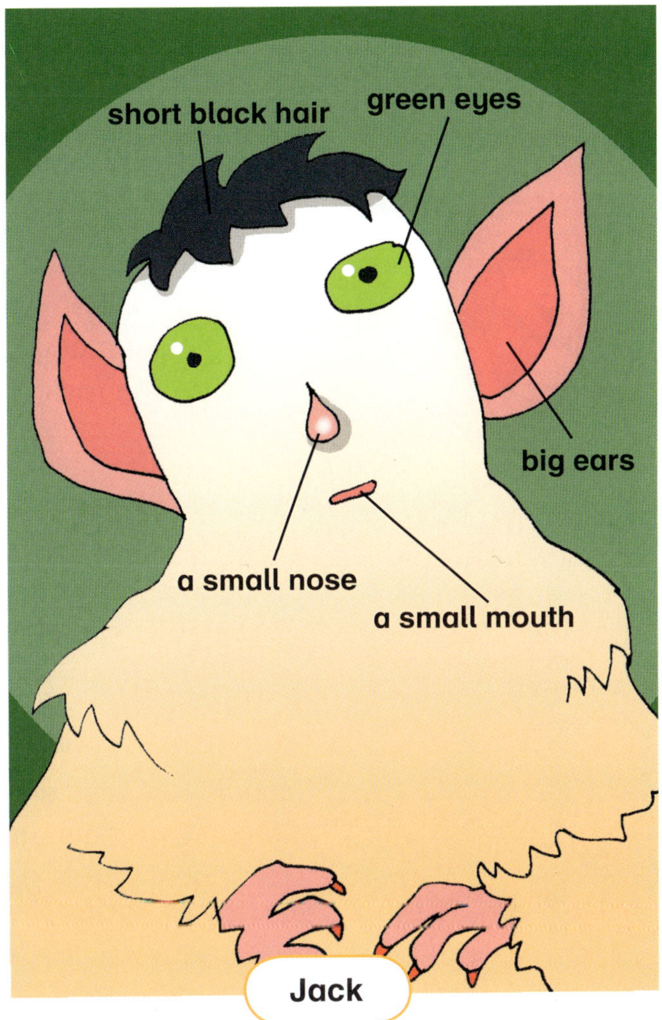

2 Test your partner.

My body

3 Listen. Sing the song.

The body rock

Let's rock, the rock, the body rock, yeah!
Listen everybody,
get ready for the rock,
the rock, the rock, the body rock, yeah!

Shake your body to the beat,
arms and hands and legs and feet,
head and hair and ears and nose,
come on, shake, from head to toes.

Boys and girls, join in, please,
touch your toes and touch your knees,
touch your ears, your nose, your lips,
clap your hands and touch your hips.

4 Look and listen. Speak.

Unit 5

My body

5 Listen. Act out.

Dialogue 1:

Mum: What's the matter with you?
Chris: I feel sick.
Mum: Have a cup of tea.
Chris: Thank you.

Dialogue 2:

Sue: Ouch!
Mum: What's the problem?
Sue: My tummy hurts.
Mum: Let's go to the doctor's.
Sue: OK.

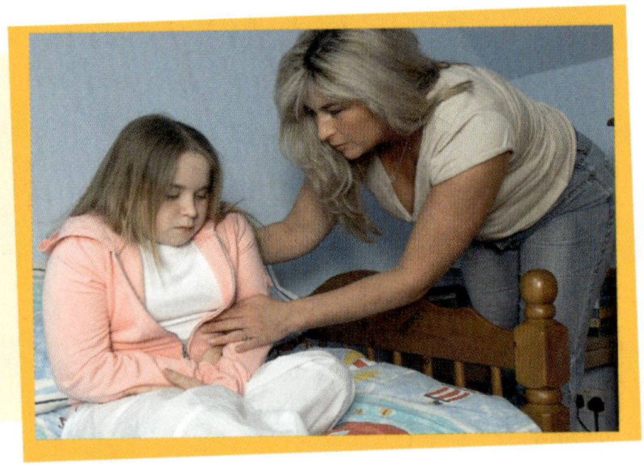

Dialogue 3:

James: Ouch!
Dad: What's the matter?
James: My left knee hurts.
Dad: Let me see.
James: Ouch! Don't touch it!
Dad: Sorry!

6 Read. Write your own text.

My text

My monster has got two red eyes
and two green ears.
My monster has got six green
teeth, five black arms and two
yellow legs.

Weather

1 Listen. What are the animals' names? Say the rhyme.

Scott	Jane	Peter	Stuart	Joe

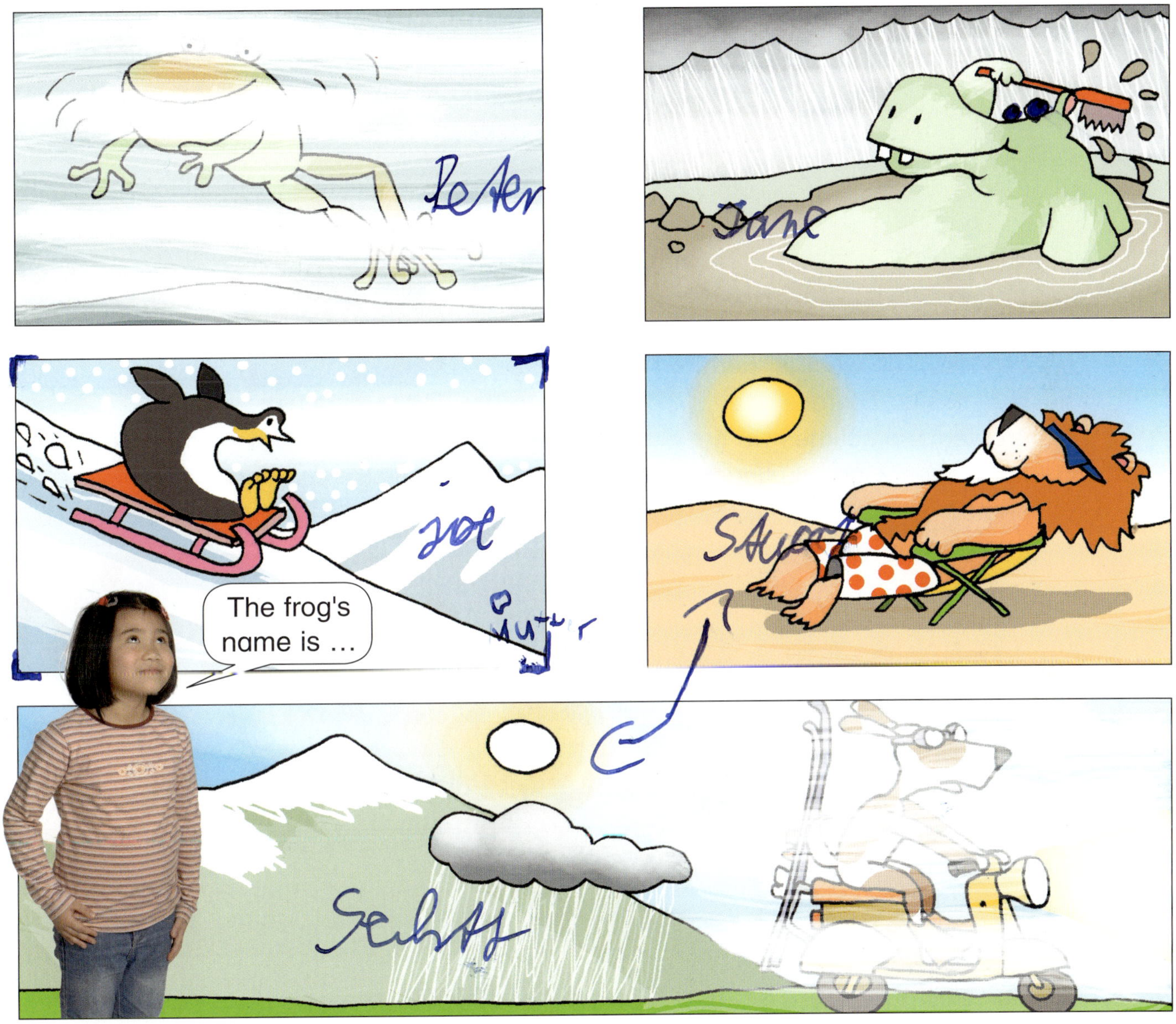

2 Listen and point.

Weather

3 Listen and read. Find the children's photos.

Hi, I'm Amy and I live in Florida. The weather here is fantastic. There is one problem: sometimes we get hurricanes. Can you find my photo?

Hello, I'm Mika and I live in Canada. There is a lot of snow in winter and it is very cold. Can you find my photo?

Weather in

Hello, I'm Judy. I live on a farm in Australia. In the summer it is very hot. Sometimes it rains in the winter. Can you find my photo?

Hi, I'm John. I live in Ireland. It rains a lot here. It rains in winter, in spring, in summer and in the autumn. It's always green here. Can you find my photo?

the world

Unit 6 Weather

4 Listen. Do the chant.

Cold and hot

It's cold outside.
Put on your jacket.
It's cold outside.
Put on your hat.
It's cold outside.
Put on your mittens.
OK, let's go.

Let's go inside.
OK, let's go.
It's hot in here.
Take off your mittens.
It's hot in here.
Take off your hat.
It's hot in here.
Take off your jacket.
Ah, that's better.

4 CD 1/53, 54, 55

5 **Make a thermometer.**

You need:
- a transparent straw
- small bottle with cold water
- a bowl
- modelling clay
- hot water

1 Put the straw in the bottle.

2 Put the modelling clay around it to hold it in place.

3 Put hot water into a bowl.

4 Put the bottle into the bowl.

Think and guess.
What happens?
Then do the experiment.

?

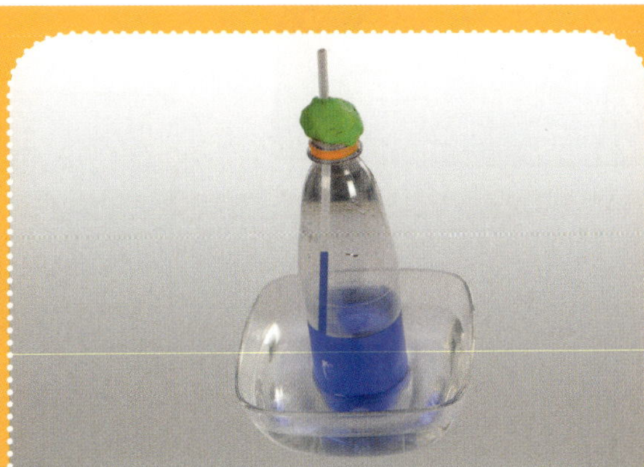

The water in the straw rises.
It's a thermometer.

Free time

1 **Listen. Do the chant. Then look and speak.**

1

2

David's week

On Monday David rides his horse,
on Tuesday he plays tennis,
on Wednesday Dave and Jennifer
sail their boat to Venice.

On Thursday David and his mum
go to the shopping mall.
On Friday David rides his bike,
and he plays volleyball.

On Saturday and Sunday
Dave's at the swimming pool.
He dives from the 5-metre board.
Hey! That is really cool!

3

4

5

6

7

Picture number 1:
It's Thursday.

1 CD 2/1, 2, 3

2 Listen and remember. Then talk about the children.

Jessica

- ride a horse
- sail a boat
- in-line skate

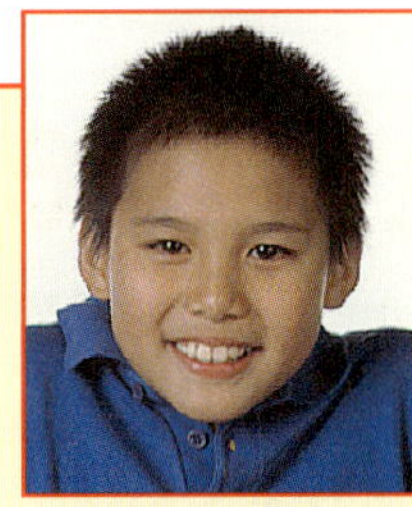

Sam

- swim
- play tennis
- ski

Anita

- swim
- skate
- play football

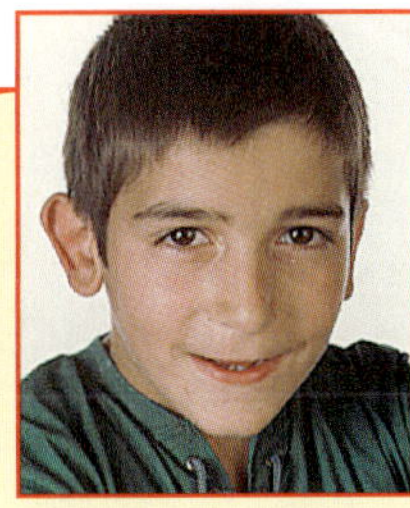

Andrew

- ride a horse
- sail a boat
- dance

3 Talk in class.

A

B

2 CD 2/4

Free time

4 Listen and read. Say who is who.

Culture Special

Children and sports

Hi, I'm Sandra. I'm from York. I can swim for one hour. I'm very good at it.

Hi! I'm Kathy. I can snowboard and skate.

I'm Claire. I'm from Cardiff. I can sail my dad's boat. I'm very good at it.

Hi, I'm Dave and I'm from London. I can dive from a 3-metre board!

I'm Christopher. I'm from Dublin. I can run 2 miles.

I'm Tony from Oxford. I can ride a unicycle. It's great fun.

5 Listen. Sing the song.

Busy Lizzy

Her name is Lizzy,
and she's so busy.
She's got so many
things to do.

She feeds the squirrels in the park,
she plays the saxophone.
She rides her bike around the town
and then she dances with a clown.

Her name is ...

She goes sailing every day,
and she plays volleyball.
She cooks spaghetti for her friends,
her busy day just never ends.

Her name is ...

6 Read. Write your own text.

My text

I can sail a boat.
I'm good at it.
I can in-line skate and
ride a unicycle.

My text

My best friend is Oliver.
He is 9. He plays football a lot.
He is very good at it.

Unit 8 Birthdays

1 Listen and point. Speak.

2 Listen. Then play a guessing game.

 1 CD 2/10 2 CD 2/11

3 Listen and read. Then speak.

4 Change the dialogue and act it out. Use these words.

hot dogs | nuts | oranges | fruit salad | cola | lemonade

5 Read. Write your own text.

My text

My birthday is in August.
Then I have a big party.
I invite ten friends.
We eat cake and sandwiches,
and drink orange juice.
We play games and listen to CDs.

Unit 9

At home

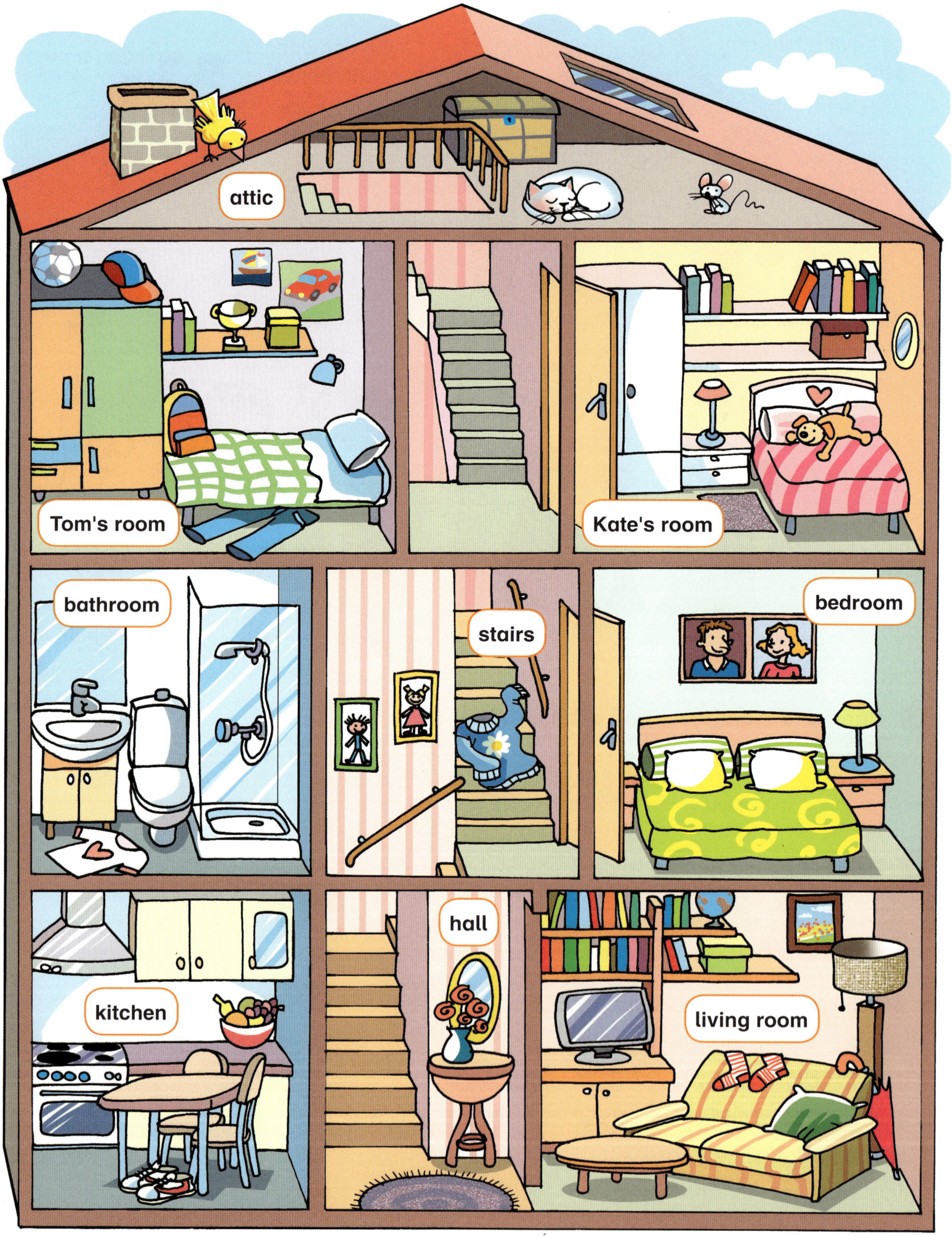

1 Play the game.

2 Look at the picture on page 38. Find the things.

Where are Tom's socks?
Where's his cap?
Where are his jeans?
Where's his schoolbag?

Where are Kate's trainers?
Where's her T-shirt?
Where's her pullover?
Where's her umbrella?

under

behind

on

next to

in

in front of

3 Ask a partner.

At home

4  **Listen and read.**

Culture Special

Living in London

I'm Rachel. I'm 9 years old and I live in London.
London is fantastic! There are lots of things you can do. There are interesting museums. There are great parks and super shops. And there are double-decker buses. Come to London and take a ride!

A London bus.

The theme park at Alton Towers has some fantastic rides! But my mum says they're scary!!

This is the London Eye. I love it! From up there the city looks great!

This is the market at Portobello Road. You can get lots of things there: clothes, shoes, fruit, vegetables and beautiful old things.

This is my favourite museum, the Natural History Museum. It has a very big fossil of a Brontosaurus.

4 CD 2/16

5 Make a desk, a chair, a bed and a wardrobe.
Listen to Simon and put the things in his room.

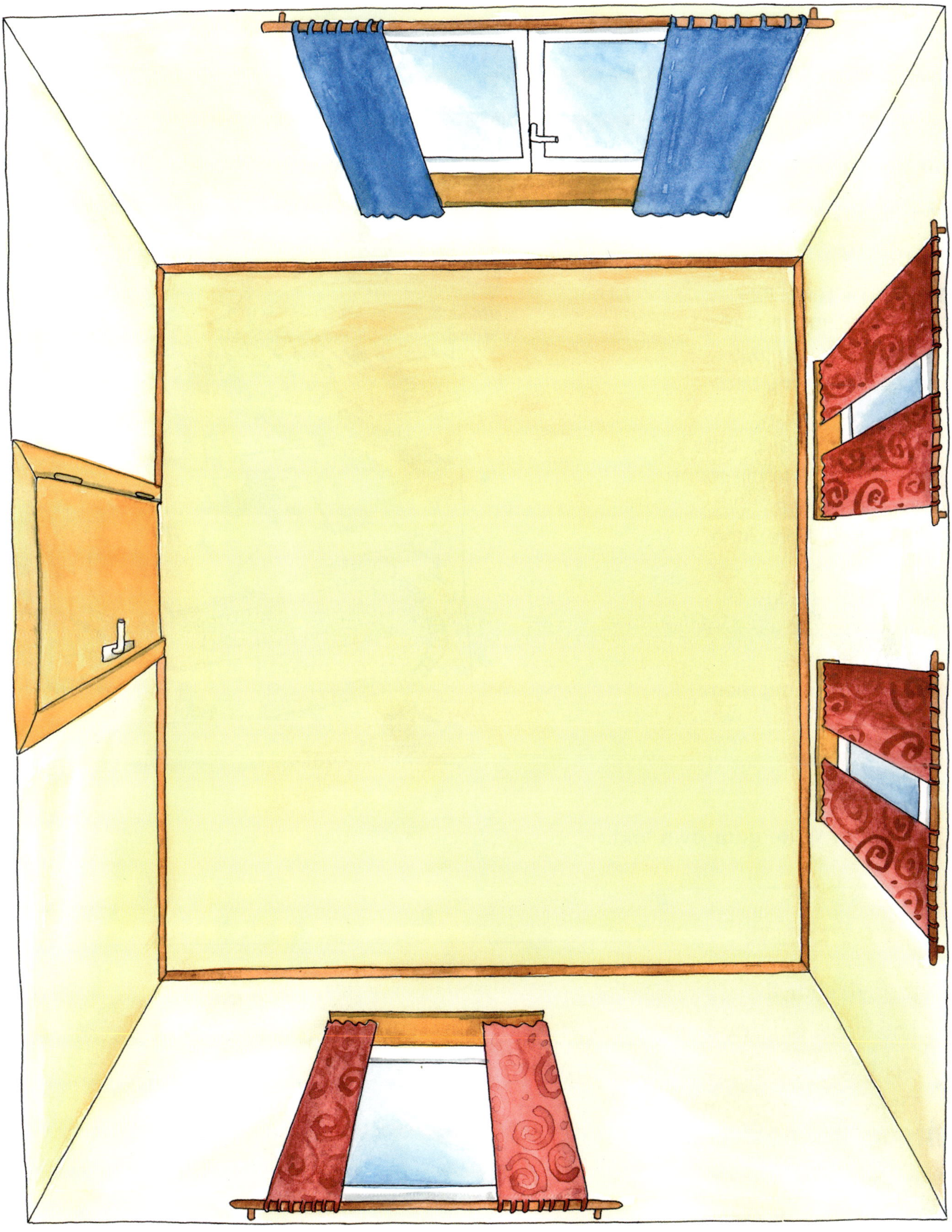

At home

6  **Listen. Sing the song.**

The racoon in my room

There's a racoon,
a little racoon,
a little racoon
in my room, oh yes!

He's drinking my milk
and he's eating my bread,
he's breaking my toys
and he's using my bed.

Please, Mum, don't come in.
There's a mess in my room.
I think my racoon
won't leave before June.

Don't tell anybody
my little racoon
is just an excuse
for the mess in my room.

7 **Read. Write your own text.**

My room

In my room there's a nice bed.
The desk is in front of the window.
Next to the desk there's a big wardrobe.
There are three posters in my room.
On the posters there are horses.

6 CD 2/18, 19

Food and drink

1 Listen and say.

Note:
☺ she likes
☹ she doesn't like

	 June	 Irene	 Kate	 Nicola
	☹	☹	☺	☺
	☹	☺	☹	☺
	☺	☺	☺	☹
	☹	☹	☹	☺
	☺	☺	☺	☹

Food and drink

2 **Listen. Sing the song.**

Luba's restaurant

Luba's is a crazy restaurant.
Luba's is the place to go.
Luba's is the place for you and me,
come here and you will see!

There is fish in your orange juice and
ice cream on your steak.
There's fruit on your pizza,
and salad on your cake!

Luba's is a crazy restaurant.
Luba's is the place to go.
Luba's is the place for you and me,
come here and you will see!

There are nuts in your tomato soup
and coffee on your pie –
and on top of your dessert
there is a fly!
Oh, no!

2 CD 2/21, 22

3 Listen and remember. What are they having?

4 How many true sentences can you make? How many lies can you make?

Mum / Dad / Linda / Benny / Max

's having

pizza / chicken / sausages / spaghetti / fish / steak

and / with

chips. / potatoes. / carrots. / a mixed salad. / peas. / beans.

And

he / she

's having

tea. / a cola. / coffee. / mineral water. / an orange juice. / lemonade.

CD 2/23

Food and drink

5 **At the restaurant.** **Listen. Then do a role play.**

 5 CD 2/26

6 Listen. Act out dialogues in class.

Girl: What have you got?

Boy: Two apples and two sandwiches.

Girl: I've got two pears. Give me an apple, please. You can have a pear.

Boy: OK. Here you are.

Girl: Thank you.

Boy: I'm very hungry.

Girl: So am I.

7 Read. Write your own text.

My text

My favourite food is pizza.
My number 2 is chicken.
My number 3 is fish.
My favourite drink is ice tea.
My number 2 is milk.
My number 3 is mineral water.

Food and drink

8 **How to make a strawberry-banana milk shake.**

You need:

- 4 cups of milk
- 1 cup of cut-up banana
- 1 cup of cut-up strawberries
- 2 teaspoons of sugar
- a blender

1 Wash the strawberries.

2 Cut them into small pieces.

3 Cut up a small banana.

4 Put the milk into a blender.

5 Add the sugar, strawberries and the banana.

6 Mix everything. Yummy!

Christmas

1 Listen and read.

Culture Special

Christmas in Britain and Australia

Hi, I'm Christina from Cambridge. This is our Christmas.

On Christmas Day we have Christmas dinner. Here you see my brother Pete, my grandma and grandpa, and my mum and dad.

This is a Christmas cracker.

This is my brother Mike. He is opening his presents on Christmas Day.

Hi, I'm Mark from Sydney.

On Christmas Day we often have a party on the beach. These are my parents and their friends.

On Christmas Eve we hang up our Christmas stockings.

Christmas

Father Christmas is hungry

A musical play in five scenes

Benny

Linda

Max

Father Christmas

Man

Mum and Dad

2  **Watch the musical play.**  **Then listen and say what's wrong.**

Benny, Linda and Max are sleeping.

Father Christmas comes into their room.

He brings some fruit for the children.

Linda and Benny wake up.

Father Christmas is angry.

He wants some pizza with onions and tomatoes.

2 CD 2/36–65

Father Christmas pays for the pizza.

Max hates pizza.

Father Christmas and Benny eat the pizza.

Mum and Dad bring tea and ice cream.

They see Father Christmas and run away.

In the end, they all play bingo.

Word list

A

a lot (PW2)	viel
about	über/von
again (PW1)	noch einmal
all	alle
always (PW1)	immer
angry (PW2)	wütend
animal (PW1)	Tier
apple (PW1)	Apfel
April	April
arm (PW2)	Arm
around	herum
attic	Dachboden
August	August
autumn	Herbst

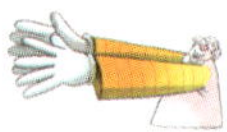

B

back (PW2)	zurück
bag	Tasche, Beutel, Tüte
ball (PW1)	Ball
bathroom (PW2)	Bad
be (am, is, are)	sein (bin, ist, sind)
beach (PW2)	Strand
beautiful	schön
bed (PW1)	Bett
bedroom	Schlafzimmer
bee (PW1)	Biene
before	vor
behind	hinter
best, better	beste/r/s, besser
big (PW1)	groß
bike (PW1)	Fahrrad
black (PW1)	schwarz
blue (PW1)	blau
board	Tafel
boat (PW1)	Boot
body (PW2)	Körper
boy	Junge
bread	Brot
break	kaputtgehen/ruinieren
breakfast (PW1)	Frühstück
bring	bringen
brother (PW2)	Bruder
brown (PW1)	braun
budgie	Wellensittich
bus (PW2)	Bus
busy (PW2)	beschäftigt
but	aber
butterfly (PW1)	Schmetterling

C

cake (PW1)	Kuchen/Torte
call (PW2)	anrufen/rufen
can (PW1)	können
cap (PW1)	Kappe
carrot (PW2)	Möhre
cat (PW1)	Katze
caterpillar	Raupe
chair (PW1)	Stuhl
cheese (PW1)	Käse
child, children (PW2)	Kind, Kinder
chocolate (PW1)	Schokolade
Christmas (PW1)	Weihnachten
city	Stadt
clap (PW2)	klatschen
clean	putzen
climb (PW2)	klettern
It's … o'clock.	Es ist … Uhr.
close (PW1)	schließen
clothes (PW2)	Kleidung
cold (PW1)	kalt
come (PW1)	kommen
cook	kochen, Koch
cool (PW1)	cool/toll
cool off	abkühlen
crazy (PW2)	verrückt
croc/crocodile (PW1)	Krokodil
cup	Tasse
cut (PW1)	schneiden

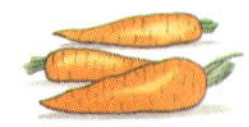

D

dad (PW1)	Vater
dance (PW2)	tanzen
danger	Gefahr
daughter	Tochter
day (PW2)	Tag
December	Dezember
desk	Schreibtisch
dessert	Nachtisch
dive (PW2)	ins Wasser springen/ tauchen
do (PW1)	tun
doctor (PW2)	Arzt
dog (PW1)	Hund
doll (PW1)	Puppe
door	Tür
down	herunter
drink	trinken
duck (PW1)	Ente

E

ear (PW1)	Ohr
eat (PW1)	essen

egg (PW1)	**Ei**
every	**jede/r/s/n**
Excuse me, ...	**Entschuldigen Sie, ...**
eye (PW1) 	**Auge**

F

face (PW1)	**Gesicht**
fair hair	**helles blondes Haar**
away	**weg**
farm (PW2)	**Bauernhof**
favourite	**Lieblings-**
February	**Februar**
feed (PW2)	**füttern**
feel (PW1)	**fühlen**
fill	**füllen**
find	**finden**
fire brigade	**Feuerwehr** 
first	**zuerst**
fish and chips (PW1)	**Fisch und Pommes Frites**
fit	**passen, fit sein**
flower (PW1) 	**Blume**
fly	**Fliege, fliegen**
fog	**Nebel**
follow	**folgen**
food (PW1)	**Essen**
foot/feet (PW2)	**Fuß/Füße**
for (PW1)	**für**
fox (PW2)	**Fuchs**
Friday	**Freitag**
friend	**Freund/Freundin**
frog (PW1)	**Frosch**
from (PW2)	**von, aus**
fruit (PW1)	**Frucht/Obst**
fun (PW2)	**Spaß**
funny (PW2)	**lustig**

G

game	**Spiel**
garden (PW2)	**Garten**
get (PW1)	**bekommen/werden/holen**
get up	**aufstehen**
girl (PW1)	**Mädchen**
give (PW1)	**geben**
go (PW1)	**gehen**
goal	**Tor**
golden	**golden**
grandma (PW2)	**Großmutter** 
grandpa (PW2)	**Großvater**
great (PW2)	**großartig**
green (PW1)	**grün**
grey (PW1)	**grau**
guinea pig	**Meerschweinchen**

H

hair (PW2) 	**Haare**
half past three	**halb** vier
hall	**Flur**
Halloween	**Halloween**
hamburger/burger	**Hamburger, Frikadelle**
hand (PW2)	**Hand** 
happy (PW2)	**glücklich**
hat (PW2)	**Hut**
hate (PW1)	**hassen**
have a snack	**einen Imbiss einnehmen**
have/has got (PW1)	**haben, hat**
he	**er**
head (PW2) 	**Kopf**
heavy	**schwer**
hedgehog	**Igel**
help (PW1)	**Hilfe, helfen**
her (PW2)	**ihr**
here (PW1)	**hier**
him	**ihm**
hippo (PW1)	**Nilpferd** 
hip	**Hüfte**
his	**sein/e/r**
at **home** (PW2)	**zu Hause**
honey (PW2)	**Honig**
horse (PW2)	**Pferd**
hot (PW2)	**heiß**
house (PW2)	**Haus**
how (PW1)	**wie**
hungry (PW1)	**hungrig**
hurry up (PW2)	**sich beeilen**
hurt (PW1)	**schmerzen**

I

I (PW1)	**ich**
ice cream (PW1)	**Eiscreme**
I've got an idea. (PW2)	**Ich habe eine Idee.**
in (PW1)	**in**
in front of 	**vor**
in-line skate	**inline skaten**
insect	**Insekt**
inside	**drinnen**
interesting	**interessant**
iron (my) shirt	**(mein) Hemd bügeln**
is (PW1)	**ist**
it (PW1)	**es**

J

jacket (PW2)	**Jacke** 
January	**Januar**
jeans	**Jeans**
join in (PW2)	**mitmachen**

Word list

juice	Saft
July	Juli
June	Juni

K

kitchen (PW1)	Küche
knee (PW1)	Knie
know	kennen, wissen

L

lamp (PW2)	Lampe
leaf/leaves	Blatt/Blätter
leave	weggehen
left	links
leg (PW1)	Bein
lemonade	Zitronenlimonade
let	lassen
like (PW1)	mögen
lion (PW1)	Löwe
lip	Lippe
listen (to)	zuhören
little	klein
live (PW2)	leben
living room	Wohnzimmer
long (PW1)	lang
look (PW1)	schauen/suchen
louse	Laus
love (PW2)	lieben, Liebe
lovely (PW1)	lieb/schön
lunch	Mittagessen

M

main course	Hauptgang
make (PW1)	machen
many (PW1)	viele
March	März
market	Markt
marry	heiraten
maths	Mathematik
May	Mai
me	mir, mich
mess	Unordnung
midnight	Mitternacht
milk (PW1)	Milch
mitten	Fäustling/Handschuh
Monday	Montag
monkey	Affe
month	Monat
morning (PW2)	Morgen
most	meist

mouse/mice (PW1)	Maus/Mäuse
mouth (PW1)	Mund
much (PW2)	viel
mum (PW1)	Mutter/Mama
must	müssen
my (PW1)	mein/e/r/s

N

necklace	Halskette
never	nie
next (to)	neben, nächste/r/s
nice (PW1)	nett
no (PW1)	nein, kein
nose (PW1)	Nase
November	November
now (PW2)	jetzt
nut (PW2)	Nuss

O

October	Oktober
of (PW1)	von
off (PW1)	hier: fort/weg
old (PW2)	alt
on, onto	auf/an, hinauf
onion (PW2)	Zwiebel
open (PW1)	aufmachen, offen
or	oder
orange	Orange
our	unser/e/s
outside (PW1)	draußen
over here/there	da/dort drüben

P

parents	Eltern
past	hier: nach
pay	bezahlen
pear (PW1)	Birne
pea	Erbse
pen	Stift
pencil case (PW1)	Federmappe
pencil (PW1)	Bleistift
penguin	Pinguin
people	Leute, Menschen
pepper (PW2)	Paprika/Pfeffer
pet (PW1)	Haustier
picture (PW1)	Bild
pie	gefüllter Kuchen
piece (PW1)	Stück
pig	Schwein
pirate	Pirat
place	Ort, Platz
play (PW1)	spielen, Aufführung

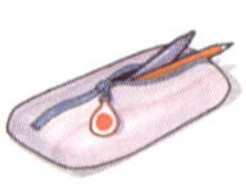

pony	**Pony**
potato (PW2)	**Kartoffel**
present (PW2)	**Geschenk**
problem	**Problem**
pull	**ziehen**
put on (PW2)	**anziehen, aufsetzen**
put	**setzen/legen/stellen**

Q

a **quarter (to 9)**	**Viertel (vor 9)**
question	**Frage**
quick/ly	**schnell**
quiet	**leise**

R

rabbit (PW1)	**Kaninchen**
racket	**Schläger**
rain (PW1)	**Regen**
rat	**Ratte**
ready	**bereit/fertig**
really (PW2)	**wirklich**
red (PW1)	**rot**
reindeer	**Rentier**
restaurant	**Restaurant**
rice	**Reis**
ride (PW2)	**reiten/fahren, Fahrt**
right (PW2)	**richtig, rechts**
roof	**Dach**
room (PW2)	**Zimmer**
rubber	**Radiergummi**
ruler	**Lineal**
run (PW1)	**rennen**

S

sad	**traurig**
sail (PW2)	**segeln**
salad	**Salat**
sandwich	**belegtes Brot**
Saturday (PW2)	**Samstag**
sausage	**Wurst**
saxophone	**Saxophone**
say (PW2)	**sagen**
We are **scared** of …	Wir **fürchten** uns vor …
scary	**gruselig**
school (PW1)	**Schule**
scissors (PW1)	**Schere**
season	**Jahreszeit**
secret	**Geheimnis**
see (PW2)	**sehen**
September	**September**
shake (PW2)	**schütteln**
she	**sie**

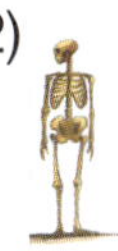

shed	**Schuppen**
shirt	**Hemd**
shoe (PW2)	**Schuh**
shoot	**schießen**
shop	**Geschäft**
short	**kurz**
shoulder (PW2)	**Schulter**
shy	**schüchtern**
sick (PW1)	**krank**
sing (PW1)	**singen**
sister	**Schwester**
skateboard (PW2)	**Skateboard**
skeleton	**Skelett**
ski	**skifahren**
skin	**Haut**
sleep (PW2)	**schlafen**
small (PW1)	**klein**
smell	**riechen**
smile	**lächeln**
snake (PW1)	**Schlange**
snow (PW1)	**Schnee**
snowboard	**snowboarden**
so	**so/also**
sock (PW2)	**Socken**
some, something	**etwas**
sometimes	**manchmal**
song (PW1)	**Lied**
I'm **sorry.** (PW1)	**Es tut mir leid.**
spaghetti (PW1)	**Spaghetti**
speak (PW1)	**sprechen/reden**
spider (PW1)	**Spinne**
spike	**Stachel**
spinach	**Spinat**
sports (PW2)	**Sport**
spring	**Frühling**
squirrel	**Eichhörnchen**
stairs	**Treppe(n)**
steak	**Steak**
stop (PW1)	**aufhören**
story (PW1)	**Geschichte**
strange	**merkwürdig**
strawberry	**Erdbeere**
sugar	**Zucker**
summer	**Sommer**
sun (PW1)	**Sonne**
Sunday	**Sonntag**
super (PW1)	**super**
sweets	**Süßigkeiten**
swim (PW2)	**schwimmen**

Word list

T

take (PW1)	**nehmen**
take off (PW2)	**ausziehen**
talk	**sprechen**
tea (PW1)	**Tee**
tell	**erzählen**
thank you	**danke**
that	**das**
their	**ihre/n**
them	**ihnen**
then	**dann**
there (PW1)	da/dort
they (PW1)	**sie**
thing (PW2)	**Ding/Sache**
think (PW1)	**denken**
thirsty (PW1)	**durstig**
this/these (PW1)	**dies/diese/r/s**
Thursday	**Donnerstag**
time (PW2)	**Zeit**
tired	**müde**
to (PW1)	**zu/nach** (örtlich)
today (PW2)	**heute**
toe (PW2)	**Zehe**
toffee	**Toffee (Sahnebonbon)**
tomato (PW2)	**Tomate**
tomorrow	**morgen**
too (PW2)	**auch**/allzu
tooth/teeth (PW1)	**Zahn/Zähne**
touch (PW1)	**berühren**
town	**Stadt**
toy (PW1)	**Spielzeug**
trainers (PW2)	**Turnschuhe**
tree (PW2)	**Baum**
trip over something	**über etwas stolpern**
true	**wahr**
try	**ausprobieren**
T-shirt (PW2)	**T-Shirt**
Tuesday	**Dienstag**
tummy (PW2)	**Bauch**
TV (television)	**Fernseher**

U

umbrella (PW1)	**Regenschirm**
under	**unter**
underground	**unter der Erde/U-Bahn**
up (PW1)	**oben, hinauf**
use	**benutzen**

V

vegetables (PW2)	**Gemüse**
Venice	**Venedig**
very (PW1)	**sehr**
volleyball	**Volleyball**

W

wake up	**aufwachen**
walk	**zu Fuß gehen**
want	**wollen**
wardrobe	**Kleiderschrank**
warm	**warm**
wash	**waschen**
watch	**Armbanduhr, zusehen**
water (PW2)	**Wasser**
we (PW1)	**wir**
weather (PW1)	**Wetter**
Wednesday	**Mittwoch**
week (PW1)	**Woche**
what (PW1)	**was**
What's the **matter?**	**Was ist los?**
when	**wann/als**
where (PW1)	**wo**
which (one)	**welch/e/r/s**
white	**weiß**
who (PW2)	**wer**
wide	**breit**
will	**werden**
window	**Fenster**
winter (PW1)	**Winter**
wish (PW2)	**wünschen/Wunsch**
with	**mit**
would	**würde**
wrong (PW2)	**falsch**

Y

year (PW2)	**Jahr**
yellow (PW1)	**gelb**
you (PW1)	**du/Sie**
your (PW1)	**dein, euer**